The Hagopian Institute, LLC has compiled the Quote   s
over 8,000 quotes, focusing mostly on short quotes th   s
of wisdom and inspiration. This particular edition o   )
every man and woman live happy and successful lives. There are nearly 900 quotes that will
help you through the best and worst times. Please enjoy, and share these quotes with your co-
workers, friends and family.

Todd Hagopian

President

The Hagopian Institute, LLC

Never do today what you can do tomorrow. Something may occur to make you regret your premature action.

Aaron Burr

And in the end it's not the years in your life that count. It's the life in your years.

Abraham Lincoln

Be sure you put your feet in the right place, then stand firm.

Abraham Lincoln

Give me six hours to chop down a tree and I will spend the first four sharpening the axe.

Abraham Lincoln

He has a right to criticize, who has a heart to help.

Abraham Lincoln

I don't like that man. I must get to know him better.

Abraham Lincoln

I will prepare and some day my chance will come.

Abraham Lincoln

Most folks are about as happy as they make their minds up to be.

Abraham Lincoln

No man has a good enough memory to be a successful liar.

Abraham Lincoln

Stand with anybody that stands right, stand with him while he is right and part with him when he goes wrong.

Abraham Lincoln

Tact is the ability to describe others as they see themselves.

Abraham Lincoln

The best thing about the future is that it comes one day at a time.

Abraham Lincoln

Things may come to those who wait, but only the things left by those who hustle.

Abraham Lincoln

To sin by silence when they should protest makes cowards of men.

Abraham Lincoln

We should be too big to take offense and too noble to give it.

Abraham Lincoln

Whatever you are, be a good one.

Abraham Lincoln

When I do good, I feel good. When I do bad, I feel bad. That's my religion.

Abraham Lincoln

You cannot escape the responsibility of tomorrow by evading it today.

Abraham Lincoln

A man should live with his superiors as he does with his fire: not too near, lest he burn; nor too far off, lest he freeze.

Albert Pike

Philosophy is a kind of journey, ever learning yet never arriving at the ideal perfection of truth.

Albert Pike

What we have done for ourselves alone dies with us; what we have done for others and the world remains and is immortal.

Albert Pike

Those who stand for nothing fall for anything.

Alexander Hamilton

Real firmness is good for anything; strut is good for nothing.

Alexander Hamilton

A well adjusted person is one who makes the same mistake twice without getting nervous.

Alexander Hamilton

A promise must never be broken.

Alexander Hamilton

All changes are more or less tinged with melancholy, for what we are leaving behind is part of ourselves.

Amelia Barr

The great difference between voyages rests not with the ships, but with the people you meet on them.

Amelia Barr

There is little success where there is little laughter.

Andrew Carnegie

No amount of ability is of the slightest avail without honor.

Andrew Carnegie

If you want to be happy, set a goal that commands your thoughts, liberates your energy, and inspires your hopes.

Andrew Carnegie

Any man worth his salt will stick up for what he believes right, but it takes a slightly better man to acknowledge instantly and without reservation that he is in error.

Andrew Jackson

Nothing is miserable unless you think it is so.

Anicius Manlius Severinus Boethius

As iron is eaten by rust, so are the envious consumed by envy.

Antisthenes

Bad men are full of repentance.

Aristotle

Change in all things is sweet.

Aristotle

Dignity consists not in possessing honors, but in the consciousness that we deserve them.

Aristotle

Fear is pain arising from the anticipation of evil.

Aristotle

Friendship is a single soul dwelling in two bodies.

Aristotle

Good habits formed at youth make all the difference.

Aristotle

Happiness depends upon ourselves.

Aristotle

He who is to be a good ruler must have first been ruled.

Aristotle

It is best to rise from life as from a banquet, neither thirsty nor drunken.

Aristotle

 Most people would rather give than get affection.

Aristotle

My best friend is the man who in wishing me well wishes it for my sake.

Aristotle

No excellent soul is exempt from a mixture of madness.

Aristotle

Probable impossibilities are to be preferred to improbable possibilities.

Aristotle

The whole is more than the sum of its parts.

Aristotle

Is boredom anything less than the sense of one's faculties slowly dying?

Arthur Helps

Wise sayings often fall on barren ground, but a kind word is never thrown away.

Arthur Helps

Just remember, once you're over the hill you begin to pick up speed.

Arthur Schopenhauer

Wealth is like sea-water; the more we drink, the thirstier we become; and the same is true of fame.

Arthur Schopenhauer

We forfeit three-quarters of ourselves in order to be like other people.

Arthur Schopenhauer

Talent hits a target no one else can hit; Genius hits a target no one else can see.

Arthur Schopenhauer

It is a clear gain to sacrifice pleasure in order to avoid pain.

Arthur Schopenhauer

Be discreet in all things, and so render it unnecessary to be mysterious.

Arthur Wellesley

Hasten slowly.

Augustus

A man of honour should never forget what he is because he sees what others are.

Baltasar Gracian

A single lie destroys a whole reputation of integrity.

Baltasar Gracian

Aspire rather to be a hero than merely appear one.

Baltasar Gracian

Be content to act, and leave the talking to others.

Baltasar Gracian

Friendship multiplies the good of life and divides the evil.

Baltasar Gracian

He that communicates his secret to another makes himself that other's slave.

Baltasar Gracian

Know or listen to those who know.

Baltasar Gracian

Let the first impulse pass, wait for the second.

Baltasar Gracian

Little said is soon amended. There is always time to add a word, never to withdraw one.

Baltasar Gracian

Never contend with a man who has nothing to lose.

Baltasar Gracian

Never do anything when you are in a temper, for you will do everything wrong.

Baltasar Gracian

Never open the door to the lesser evil, for other and greater ones invariably slink in after it.

Baltasar Gracian

Respect yourself if you would have others respect you.

Baltasar Gracian

The things we remember best are those better forgotten.

Baltasar Gracian

Friendship is an arrangement by which we undertake to exchange small favors for big ones.

Baron de Montesquieu

The less men think, the more they talk.

Baron de Montesquieu

I have striven not to laugh at human actions, not to weep at them, nor to hate them, but to understand them.

Baruch Spinoza

Happiness is a virtue, not its reward.

Baruch Spinoza

All things excellent are as difficult as they are rare.

Baruch Spinoza

The secret of success is constancy to purpose

Benjamin Disraeli

The secret of success is constancy to purpose

Benjamin Franklin

Work as if you were to live a hundred years. Pray as if you were to die tomorrow

Benjamin Franklin

Who is rich? He that rejoices in his portion.

Benjamin Franklin

When you're finished changing, you're finished.

Benjamin Franklin

When in doubt, don't.

Benjamin Franklin

Whatever is begun in anger ends in shame.

Benjamin Franklin

Those that won't be counseled can't be helped.

Benjamin Franklin

The worst wheel of the cart makes the most noise.

Benjamin Franklin

The doors of wisdom are never shut.

Benjamin Franklin

The definition of insanity is doing the same thing over and over and expecting different results.

Benjamin Franklin

Tell me and I forget. Teach me and I remember. Involve me and I learn.

Benjamin Franklin

Take time for all things: great haste makes great waste.

Benjamin Franklin

Speak ill of no man, but speak all the good you know of everybody.

Benjamin Franklin

Some people die at 25 and aren't buried until 75.

Benjamin Franklin

Rather go to bed with out dinner than to rise in debt

Benjamin Franklin

One today is worth two tomorrows.

Benjamin Franklin

Never leave that till tomorrow which you can do today.

Benjamin Franklin

Never confuse motion with action.

Benjamin Franklin

If a man empties his purse into his head, no one can take it from him.

Benjamin Franklin

If a man could have half of his wishes, he would double his troubles.

Benjamin Franklin

Honesty is the best policy.

Benjamin Franklin

He who falls in love with himself will have no rivals.

Benjamin Franklin

He that rises late must trot all day.

Benjamin Franklin

He that composes himself is wiser than he that composes a book.

Benjamin Franklin

Half a truth is often a great lie.

Benjamin Franklin

Either write something worth reading or do something worth writing.

Benjamin Franklin

Do not fear mistakes. You will know failure. Continue to reach out.

Benjamin Franklin

Beware of little expenses. A small leak will sink a great ship.

Benjamin Franklin

Be slow in choosing a friend, slower in changing.

Benjamin Franklin

An investment in knowledge pays the best interest.

Benjamin Franklin

A penny saved is a penny earned.

Benjamin Franklin

A man wrapped up in himself makes a very small bundle.

Benjamin Franklin

Well done is better than well said.

Benjamin Franklin

Employ thy time well, if thou meanest to get leisure.

Benjamin Franklin

He that is of the opinion money will do everything may well be suspected of doing everything for money.

Benjamin Franklin

Hide not your talents, they for use were made. What's a sun-dial in the shade?

Benjamin Franklin

You may delay, but time will not.

Benjamin Franklin

He that lives upon hope will die fasting.

Benjamin Franklin

Be slow in choosing a friend, slower in changing.

Benjamin Franklin

A man wrapped up in himself makes a very small bundle.

Benjamin Franklin

Having been poor is no shame, but being ashamed of it, is.

Benjamin Franklin

Wish not so much to live long as to live well.

Benjamin Franklin

Never leave that till tomorrow which you can do today.

Benjamin Franklin

Glass, china and reputation are easily cracked, and never well mended.

Benjamin Franklin

He that can have patience can have what he will.

Benjamin Franklin

Many people die at twenty five and aren't buried until they are seventy five.

Benjamin Franklin

If a man could have half of his wishes, he would double his troubles.

Benjamin Franklin

One today is worth two tomorrows.

Benjamin Franklin

Lost time is never found again.

Benjamin Franklin

Energy and persistence conquer all things.

Benjamin Franklin

A slip of the foot you may soon recover, but a slip of the tongue you may never get over.

Benjamin Franklin

☆ *Do not anticipate trouble, or worry about what may never happen.*

Benjamin Franklin

Take time for all things: great haste makes great waste.

Benjamin Franklin

An investment in knowledge always pays the best interest.

Benjamin Franklin

Be civil to all; sociable to many; familiar with few; friend to one; enemy to none.

Benjamin Franklin

The bud of victory is always in the truth.

Benjamin Harrison

 None are so empty as those who are full of themselves.

Benjamin Whichcote

Seek not good from without: seek it within yourselves, or you will never find it.

Bertha Von Suttner

Truth will lose its credit, if delivered by a person that has none.

Bishop Robert Smith

Passion is the drunkenness of the mind.

Bishop Robert Smith

If there be any truer measure of a man than by what he does, it must be by what he gives.

Bishop Robert Smith

Defeat should never be a source of discouragement, but rather a fresh stimulus.

Bishop Robert Smith

Eloquence is a painting of the thoughts.

Blaise Pascal

Few friendships would survive if each one knew what his friend says of him behind his back.

Blaise Pascal

 It is not good to be too free. It is not good to have everything one wants.

Blaise Pascal

Kind words do not cost much. Yet they accomplish much.

Blaise Pascal

Noble deeds that are concealed are most esteemed.

Blaise Pascal

The heart has its reasons of which reason knows nothing.

Blaise Pascal

Education is the power to think clearly, the power to act well in the worlds work, and the power to appreciate life.

Brigham Young

Honest hearts produce honest actions.

Brigham Young

It is wise for us to forget our troubles, there are always new ones to replace them.

Brigham Young

Love the giver more than the gift.

Brigham Young

We should never permit ourselves to do anything that we are not willing to see our children do.

Brigham Young

Three things cannot be long hidden: the sun, the moon, and the truth.

Buddha

An idea that is developed and put into action is more important than an idea that exists only as an idea.

Buddha

A jug fills drop by drop.

Buddha

All that we are is the result of what we have thought. The mind is everything. What we think we become.

Buddha

Better than a thousand hollow words, is one word that brings peace.

Buddha

Chaos is inherent in all compounded things. Strive on with diligence.

Buddha

Do not dwell in the past, do not dream of the future, concentrate the mind on the present moment.

Buddha

It is a man's own mind, not his enemy or foe, that lures him to evil ways.

Buddha

The mind is everything. What you think you become.

Buddha

The tongue like a sharp knife... Kills without drawing blood.

Buddha

There are only two mistakes one can make along the road to truth; not going all the way, and not starting.

Buddha

Those who are free of resentful thoughts surely find peace.

Buddha

Thousands of candles can be lighted from a single candle, and the life of the candle will not be shortened. Happiness never decreases by being shared.

Buddha

To be idle is a short road to death and to be diligent is a way of life; foolish people are idle, wise people are diligent.

Buddha

We are shaped by our thoughts; we become what we think. When the mind is pure, joy follows like a shadow that never leaves.

Buddha

Whatever words we utter should be chosen with care for people will hear them and be influenced by them for good or ill.

Buddha

You will not be punished for your anger, you will be punished by your anger.

Buddha

I have never been hurt by what I have not said.

Calvin Coolidge

If you see ten troubles coming down the road, you can be sure that nine will run into the ditch before they reach you.

Calvin Coolidge

Heroism is not only in the man, but in the occasion.

Calvin Coolidge

There is no dignity quite so impressive, and no one independence quite so important, as living within your means.

Calvin Coolidge

Nothing in the world can take the place of Persistence. Talent will not; nothing is more common than unsuccessful men with talent. Genius will not; unrewarded genius is almost a proverb. Education will not; the world is full of educated derelicts. Persistence and determination alone are omnipotent. The slogan 'Press On' has solved and always will solve the problems of the human race.

Calvin Coolidge

We cannot do everything at once, but we can do something at once.

Calvin Coolidge

Don't expect to build up the weak by pulling down the strong.

Calvin Coolidge

Knowledge comes, but wisdom lingers.

Calvin Coolidge

Those who trust to chance must abide by the results of chance.

Calvin Coolidge

It takes a great man to be a good listener.

Calvin Coolidge

Perhaps one of the most important accomplishments of my administration has been minding my own business.

Calvin Coolidge

 I praise loudly. I blame softly.

Catherine the Great

You will never find time for anything. If you want time you must make it.

Charles Buxton

The rule in carving holds good as to criticism; never cut with a knife what you can cut with a spoon.

Charles Buxton

In life, as in chess, forethought wins.

Charles Buxton

You have to study a great deal to know a little.

Charles de Secondat

 Not to be loved is a misfortune, but it is an insult to be loved no longer.

Charles de Secondat

Life was given to me as a favor, so I may abandon it when it is one no longer.

Charles de Secondat

No one is useless in this world who lightens the burdens of another.

Charles Dickens

Have a heart that never hardens, and a temper that never tires, and a touch that never hurts

Charles Dickens

An idea, like a ghost, must be spoken to a little before it will explain itself.

Charles Dickens

Annual income twenty pounds, annual expenditure nineteen six, result happiness.

Charles Dickens

It was the best of times, it was the worst of times.

Charles Dickens

No one is useless in the world who lightens the burden of it for anyone else.

Charles Dickens

Vices are sometimes only virtues carried to excess!

Charles Dickens

He who does not bellow the truth when he knows the truth makes himself the accomplice of liars and forgers.

Charles Peguy

Love is rarer than genius itself. And friendship is rarer than love.

Charles Peguy

We must always tell what we see. Above all, and this is more difficult, we must always see what we see.

Charles Peguy

Make 'em laugh; make 'em cry; make 'em wait.

Charles Reade

The joys we expect are not so bright, nor the troubles so dark as we fancy they will be.

Charles Reade

Better to be without logic than without feeling.

Charlotte Bronte

I feel monotony and death to be almost the same.

Charlotte Bronte

A man who would not love his father's grave is worse than a wild animal.

Chief Joseph

I will speak with a straight tongue

Chief Joseph

It does not require many words to speak the truth.

Chief Joseph

The earth is the mother of all people, and all people should have equal rights upon it.

Chief Joseph

The true worth of an experimenter consists in his pursuing not only what he seeks in his experiment, but also what he did not seek.

Claude Bernard

Say not always what you know, but always know what you say

Claudius

To do nothing evil is good; to wish nothing evil is better.

Claudius

No matter how busy you may think you are, you must find time for reading, or surrender yourself to self-chosen ignorance.

Confucius

A superior man is modest in his speech, but exceeds in his actions.

Confucius

Before you embark on a journey of revenge, dig two graves.

Confucius

When you see a man of worth, think of how you may emulate him. When you see one who is unworthy, examine yourself.

Confucius

Better a diamond with a flaw than a pebble without.

Confucius

Success depends upon previous preparation, and without such preparation there is sure to be failure.

Confucius

You cannot open a book without learning something.

Confucius

If a man takes no thought about what is distant, he will find sorrow near at hand.

Confucius

Forget injuries, never forget kindnesses.

Confucius

What you do not want done to yourself, do not do to others.

Confucius

When anger rises, think of the consequences.

Confucius

The man of virtue makes the difficulty to be overcome his first business, and success only a subsequent consideration.

Confucius

By three methods we may learn wisdom: First, by reflection, which is noblest; Second, by imitation, which is easiest; and third by experience, which is the bitterest.

Confucius

Men's natures are alike, it is their habits that carry them far apart.

Confucius

It does not matter how slowly you go so long as you do not stop.

Confucius

He who speaks without modesty will find it difficult to make his words good.

Confucius

Choose a job you love, and you will never have to work a day in your life.

Confucius

I hear and I forget. I see and I remember. I do and I understand.

Confucius

Wherever you go, go with all your heart.

Confucius

And remember, no matter where you go, there you are.

Confucius

Do not impose on others what you yourself do not desire.

Confucius

He who learns but does not think, is lost! He who thinks but does not learn is in great danger.

Confucius

I hear and I forget. I see and I remember. I do and I understand.

Confucius

Learning without thought is labor lost; thought without learning is perilous.

Confucius

Life is really simple, but we insist on making it complicated.

Confucius

Never contract friendship with a man that is not better than thyself.

Confucius

Only the wisest and stupidest of men never change.

Confucius

Real knowledge is to know the extent of one's ignorance.

Confucius

The cautious seldom err.

Confucius

The superior man acts before he speaks, and afterwards speaks according to his action.

Confucius

To be wronged is nothing unless you continue to remember it.

Confucius

Virtue is not left to stand alone. He who practices it will have neighbors.

Confucius

We should feel sorrow, but not sink under its oppression.

Confucius

What you do not want done to yourself, do not do to others.

Confucius

When anger rises, think of the consequences.

Confucius

I don't care half so much about making money as I do about making my point, and coming out ahead.

Cornelius Vanderbilt

Our opportunities to do good are our talents

Cotton Mather

A wise man proportions his belief to the evidence.

David Hume

Everything in the world is purchased by labor.

David Hume

Truth springs from argument amongst friends.

David Hume

By desiring little, a poor man makes himself rich.

Democritus

Good means not merely not to do wrong, but rather not to desire to do wrong.

Democritus

Hope of ill gain is the beginning of loss.

Democritus

It is better to destroy one's own errors than those of others.

Democritus

It is greed to do all the talking but not to want to listen at all.

Democritus

Our sins are more easily remembered than our good deeds.

Democritus

Throw moderation to the winds, and the greatest pleasures bring the greatest pains.

Democritus

A nail is driven out by another nail. Habit is overcome by habit.

Desiderius Erasmus

Concealed talent brings no reputation.

Desiderius Erasmus

Don't give your advice before you are called upon.

Desiderius Erasmus

Humility is truth.

Desiderius Erasmus

Prevention is better than cure.

Desiderius Erasmus

Time takes away the grief of men.

Desiderius Erasmus

It is astonishing what a lot of odd minutes one can catch during the day, if one really sets about it.

Dinah Maria Mulock

Blushing is the color of virtue.

Diogenes

He has the most who is most content with the least.

Diogenes

I am not an Athenian or a Greek, but a citizen of the world.

Diogenes

I know nothing, except the fact of my ignorance.

Diogenes

I threw my cup away when I saw a child drinking from his hands at the trough.

Diogenes

We have two ears and one tongue so that we would listen more and talk less.

Diogenes

Wise kings generally have wise counselors; and he must be a wise man himself who is capable of distinguishing one.

Diogenes

The blessings we evoke for another descend upon ourselves.

Edmund Gibson

I may err in judgment, but I hope not in intention.

Edward Blake

I am indeed rich, since my income is superior to my expenses, and my expense is equal to my wishes.

Edward Gibbon

 I never make the mistake of arguing with people for whose opinions I have no respect.

Edward Gibbon

The winds and the waves are always on the side of the ablest navigators.

Edward Gibbon

Every man should make up his own mind that if he expect to succeed, he must give an honest return for the other man's dollar.

Edward Harriman

The friend is the man who knows all about you, and still likes you.

Elbert Hubbard

A failure is a man who has blundered, but is not able to cash in the experience.

Elbert Hubbard

I would rather be able to appreciate things I can not have than to have things I am not able to appreciate.

Elbert Hubbard

Do your work with your whole heart, and you will succeed - there's so little competition.

Elbert Hubbard

Get happiness out of your work or you may never know what happiness is.

Elbert Hubbard

He has achieved success who has worked well, laughed often, and loved much.

Elbert Hubbard

Live truth instead of professing it.

Elbert Hubbard

There is no failure except in no longer trying.

Elbert Hubbard

An ounce of loyalty is worth a pound of cleverness.

Elbert Hubbard

The greatest mistake you can make in life is continually fearing that you'll make one.

Elbert Hubbard

A little credulity helps one on through life very smoothly.

Elizabeth Gaskell

The cloud never comes from the quarter of the horizon from which we watch for it.

Elizabeth Gaskell

The stone often recoils on the head of the thrower.

Elizabeth I

The past cannot be cured.

Elizabeth I

If I cannot overwhelm with my quality, I will overwhelm with my quantity.

Emile Zola

If you ask me what I came into this life to do, I will tell you: I came to live out loud.

Emile Zola

If I could I would always work in silence and obscurity, and let my efforts be known by their results.

Emily Bronte

The nature of God is a circle of which the center is everywhere and the circumference is nowhere.

Empedocles

Control thy passions lest they take vengence on thee.

Epictetus

First learn the meaning of what you say, and then speak.

Epictetus

If evil be spoken of you and it be true, correct yourself, if it be a lie, laugh at it.

Epictetus

If one oversteps the bounds of moderation, the greatest pleasures cease to please.

Epictetus

If thy brother wrongs thee, remember not so much his wrong-doing, but more than ever that he is thy brother.

Epictetus

♪

If you wish to be a writer, write.

Epictetus

It's not what happens to you, but how you react to it that matters.

Epictetus

Know, first, who you are, and then adorn yourself accordingly.

Epictetus

Make the best use of what is in your power, and take the rest as it happens.

Epictetus

Men are disturbed not by things, but by the view which they take of them.

Epictetus

No great thing is created suddenly.

Epictetus

Wealth consists not in having great possessions, but in having few wants.

Epictetus

It is not so much our friends' help that helps us, as the confidence of their help.

Epictetus

The art of living well and the art of dying well are one.

Epictetus

When people complain of life, it is almost always because they have asked impossible things of it.

Ernest Renan

Virtue often trips and falls on the sharp-edges rock of poverty.

Eugene Sue

Idleness is to the human mind like rust to iron.

Ezra Cornell

Since there is nothing so well worth having as friends, never lose a chance to make them

Francesco Guicciardini

Anger makes dull men witty, but it keeps them poor.

Francis Bacon

For also knowledge itself is power.

Francis Bacon

God hangs the greatest weights upon the smallest wires.

Francis Bacon

The fortune which nobody sees makes a person happy and unenvied.

Francis Bacon

The worst solitude is to have no real friendships.

Francis Bacon

Wisdom denotes the pursuing of the best ends by the best means.

Francis Hutcheson

What is the good of experience if you do not reflect?

Frederick II

He who defends everything defends nothing.

Frederick II

Kindness has converted more sinners than zeal, eloquence, or learning.

Frederick William Faber

Every moment of resistance to temptation is a victory.

Frederick William Faber

A friend should be a master at guessing and keeping still: you must not want to see everything.

Friedrich Nietzsche

Character is determined more by the lack of certain experiences than by those one has had.

Friedrich Nietzsche

One may sometimes tell a lie, but the grimace that accompanies it tells the truth.

Friedrich Nietzsche

That which does not kill us makes us stronger.

Friedrich Nietzsche

To forget one's purpose is the commonest form of stupidity.

Friedrich Nietzsche

Much unhappiness has come into the world because of bewilderment and things left unsaid

Fyodor Dostoevsky

There is no subject so old that something new cannot be said about it.

Fyodor Dostoevsky

To live without Hope is to Cease to live.

Fyodor Dostoevsky

The same principles which at first view lead to skepticism, pursued to a certain point, bring men back to common sense.

George Berkeley

We have first raised a dust and then complain we cannot see.

George Berkeley

Attitudes are more important than facts.

George Macdonald

The best preparation for the future is the present well seen to, and the last duty done.

George Macdonald

The first thing a kindness deserves is acceptance, the second, transmission.

George Macdonald

The principle part of faith is patience.

George Macdonald

There are thousands willing to do great things for one willing to do a small thing.

George Macdonald

To have what we want is riches; but to be able to do without is power.

George Macdonald

Where there is no choice, we do well to make no difficulty.

George Macdonald

Always imitate the behavior of the winners when you lose.

George Meredith

Don't just count your years, make your years count.

George Meredith

The well of true wit is truth itself.

George Meredith

There is only one happiness in life, to love and be loved.

George Sand

We cannot tear out a single page of our life, but we can throw the whole book in the fire.

George Sand

Most men make little use of their speech than to give evidence against their own understanding.

George Savile

Many men swallow the being cheated, but no man can ever endure to chew it.

George Savile

A man may dwell so long upon a thought that it may take him prisoner.

George Savile

Men's fame is like their hair, which grows after they are dead, and with just as little use to them.

George Villiers

Labor to keep alive in your breast that little spark of celestial fire, called conscience.

George Washington

Associate with men of good quality if you esteem your own reputation; for it is better to be alone than in bad company.

George Washington

If the freedom of speech is taken away then dumb and silent we may be led, like sheep to the slaughter.

George Washington

Time takes all and gives all.

Giordano Bruno

Anything becomes interesting if you look at it long enough.

Gustave Flaubert

If at first you do succeed - try to hide your astonishment.

Harry Banks

An error is the more dangerous in proportion to the degree of truth which it contains.

Henri Frederic Amiel

Destiny has two ways of crushing us - by refusing our wishes and by fulfilling them.

Henri Frederic Amiel

Man becomes man only by his intelligence, but he is man only by his heart.

Henri Frederic Amiel

Work while you have the light. You are responsible for the talent that has been entrusted to you.

Henri Frederic Amiel

Friends are born, not made.

Henry B. Adams

The language of friendship is not words but meanings.

Henry David Thoreau

Cultivate the habit of early rising. It is unwise to keep the head long on a level with the feet.

Henry David Thoreau

Be true to your work, your word, and your friend.

Henry David Thoreau

Things do not change; we change.

Henry David Thoreau

If you make money your god, it will plague you like the devil.

Henry Fielding

A single conversation across the table with a wise man is better than ten years mere study of books.

Henry Wadsworth Longfellow

Perseverance is a great element of success. If you only knock long enough and loud enough at the gate, you are sure to wake up somebody.

Henry Wadsworth Longfellow

However things may seem, no evil thing is success and no good thing is failure.

Henry Wadsworth Longfellow

He that respects himself is safe from others. He wears a coat of mail that none can pierce.

Henry Wadsworth Longfellow

A thought often makes us hotter than a fire.

Henry Wadsworth Longfellow

Sometimes we may learn more from a man's errors, than from his virtues.

Henry Wadsworth Longfellow

Into each life some rain must fall.

Henry Wadsworth Longfellow

Hold yourself responsible for a higher standard than anybody expects of you. Never excuse yourself.

Henry Ward Beecher

It is one of the severest tests of friendship to tell your friend his faults. So to love a man that you cannot bear to see a stain upon him, and to speak painful truth through loving words, that is friendship.

Henry Ward Beecher

He is rich or poor according to what he is, not according to what he has.

Henry Ward Beecher

A person without a sense of humor is like a wagon without springs. It's jolted by every pebble on the road.

Henry Ward Beecher

The true secret of giving advice is, after you have honestly given it, to be perfectly indifferent whether it is taken or not, and never persist in trying to set people right.

Henry Ward Beecher

Good nature is worth more than knowledge, more than money, more than honor, to the persons who possess it.

Henry Ward Beecher

The difference between perseverance and obstinacy is that one comes from a strong will, and the other from a strong won't.

Henry Ward Beecher

A helping word to one in trouble is often like a switch on a railroad track, - but one inch between wreck and smooth-rolling prosperity.

Henry Ward Beecher

The art of being happy lies in the power of extracting happiness from common things.

Henry Ward Beecher

Our best successes often come after our greatest disappointments.

Henry Ward Beecher

Every man should keep a fair-sized cemetery in which to bury the faults of his friends.

Henry Ward Beecher

A man's character is his fate.

Heraclitus

Justice will overtake fabricators of lies and false witnesses.

Heraclitus

Our envy always lasts longer than the happiness of those we envy.

Heraclitus

The eyes are more exact witnesses than the ears.

Heraclitus

Our lives are universally shortened by our ignorance.

Herbert Spencer

How often misused words generate misleading thoughts.

Herbert Spencer

Better sleep with a sober cannibal than a drunken Christian.

Herman Melville

I am, as I am; whether hideous, or handsome, depends upon who is made judge.

Herman Melville

It is not down in any map; true places never are.

Herman Melville

There are some enterprises in which a careful disorderliness is the true method.

Herman Melville

There is nothing namable but that some men will, or undertake to, do it for pay.

Herman Melville

They talk of the dignity of work. The dignity is in leisure.

Herman Melville

To be called one thing, is oftentimes to be another.

Herman Melville

Of all possessions a friend is the most precious.

Herodotus

A good marriage would be between a blind wife and a deaf husband.

Honore de Balzac

Power is not revealed by striking hard or often, but by striking true.

Honore de Balzac

A good husband is never the first to go to sleep at night or the last to awake in the morning.

Honore de Balzac

Excess of joy is harder to bear than any amount of sorrow.

Honore de Balzac

It is easy to sit up and take notice, What is difficult is getting up and taking action.

Honore de Balzac

The more one judges, the less one loves.

Honore de Balzac

There is no such thing as a great talent without great will power.

Honore de Balzac

Those who spend too fast never grow rich.

Honore de Balzac

Be moderate in everything, including moderation.

Horace Porter

Time is everything; five minutes make the difference between victory and defeat.

Horatio Nelson

Always recognize that human individuals are ends, and do not use them as means to your end.

Immanuel Kant

By a lie, a man... annihilates his dignity as a man.

Immanuel Kant

It is beyond a doubt that all our knowledge that begins with experience.

Immanuel Kant

Science is organized knowledge. Wisdom is organized life.

Immanuel Kant

Thoughts without content are empty, intuitions without concepts are blind.

Immanuel Kant

Well-arranged time is the surest mark of a well-arranged mind.

Isaac Pitman

Acquaint yourself with your own ignorance.

Isaac Watts

It is a trick among the dishonest to offer sacrifices that are not needed, or not possible, to avoid making those that are required.

Ivan Goncharov

I agree with no one's opinion. I have some of my own.

Ivan Turgenev

The word tomorrow was invented for indecisive people and for children.

Ivan Turgenev

Go as far as you can see; when you get there, you'll be able to see farther.

J.P. Morgan

A bone to the dog is not charity. Charity is the bone shared with the dog, when you are just as hungry as the dog.

Jack London

Life is not a matter of holding good cards, but sometimes, playing a poor hand well.

Jack London

You can't wait for inspiration. You have to go after it with a club.

Jack London

As we advance in life, we learn the limits of our abilities.

James Anthony Froude

In everyday things the law of sacrifice takes the form of positive duty.

James Anthony Froude

The essence of greatness is neglect of the self.

James Anthony Froude

He who has provoked the lash of wit, cannot complain that he smarts from it.

James Boswell

Three-fourths of the mistakes a man makes are made because he does not really know what he thinks he knows.

James Bryce

If wrinkles must be written on our brows, let them not be written upon the heart. The spirit should never grow old.

James Garfield

A man is accountable to no person for his doings.

James Otis

A man's house is his castle.

James Otis

Let the consequences be what they will, I am determined to proceed.

James Otis

A vain man finds it wise to speak good or ill of himself; a modest man does not talk of himself.

Jean de la Bruyere

One must laugh before one is happy, or one may die without ever laughing at all.

Jean de la Bruyere

One seeks to make the loved one entirely happy, or, if that cannot be, entirely wretched.

Jean de la Bruyere

Politeness makes one appear outwardly as they should be within.

Jean de la Bruyere

The pleasure we feel in criticizing robs us from being moved by very beautiful things.

Jean de la Bruyere

We can recognize the dawn and the decline of love by the uneasiness we feel when alone together.

Jean de la Bruyere

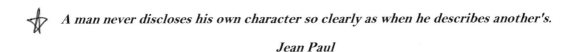 *A man never discloses his own character so clearly as when he describes another's.*

Jean Paul

Do not wait for extraordinary circumstances to do good action; try to use ordinary situations.

Jean Paul

Good actions ennoble us, we are the sons of our own deeds.

Jean Paul

When something an affliction happens to you, you either let it defeat you, or you defeat it.

Jean-Jacques Rousseau

It is too difficult to think nobly when one thinks only of earning a living.

Jean-Jacques Rousseau

Gratitude is a duty which ought to be paid, but which none have a right to expect.

Jean-Jacques Rousseau

It is the greatest good to the greatest number of people which is the measure of right and wrong.

Jeremy Bentham

Stretching his hand up to reach the stars, too often man forgets the flowers at his feet.

Jeremy Bentham

You are not very good if you are not better than your best friends imagine you to be.

Johann Kaspar Lavater

Who makes quick use of the moment is a genius of prudence.

Johann Kaspar Lavater

Trust him not with your secrets, who, when left alone in your room, turns over your papers.

Johann Kaspar Lavater

The public seldom forgive twice.

Johann Kaspar Lavater

He who seldom speaks, and with one calm well-timed word can strike dumb the loquacious, is a genius or a hero.

Johann Kaspar Lavater

 Don't speak evil of someone if you don't know for certain, and if you do know ask yourself, why am I telling it?

Johann Kaspar Lavater

I have always thought the actions of men the best interpreters of their thoughts.

John Locke

There cannot be greater rudeness than to interrupt another in the current of his discourse.

John Locke

What worries you, masters you.

John Locke

To listen well is as powerful a means of communication and influence as to talk well.

John Marshall

All men profess honesty as long as they can. To believe all men honest would be folly. To believe none so is something worse.

John Quincy Adams

All good things which exist are the fruits of originality.

John Stuart Mill

What distinguishes the majority of men from the few is their inability to act according to their beliefs.

John Stuart Mill

To be able to bear provocation is an argument of great reason, and to forgive it of a great mind.

John Tillotson

The art of using deceit and cunning grow continually weaker and less effective to the user.

John Tillotson

Ignorance and inconsideration are the two great causes of the ruin of mankind.

John Tillotson

A good word is an easy obligation; but not to speak ill requires only our silence, which costs us nothing.

John Tillotson

Popularity, I have always thought, may aptly be compared to a coquette - the more you woo her, the more apt is she to elude your embrace.

John Tyler

Courtesies cannot be borrowed like snow shovels; you must have some of your own.

John Wanamaker

Courtesy is the one coin you can never have too much of or be stingy with.

John Wanamaker

 Never read a book through merely because you have begun it.

John Witherspoon

I believe that in the end truth will conquer.

John Wycliffe

A wise man should have money in his head, but not in his heart.

Jonathan Swift

One of the best rules in conversation is, never to say a thing which any of the company can reasonably wish had been left unsaid.

Jonathan Swift

It is a sin not to do what one is capable of doing.

Jose Marti

A grain of poetry suffices to season a century.

Jose Marti

Charm is a product of the unexpected.

Jose Marti

Other famous men, those of much talk and few deeds, soon evaporate. Action is the dignity of greatness.

Jose Marti

Learn to think impartially.

Joseph Chamberlain

Be like a postage stamp. Stick to one thing until you get there.

Josh Billings

Flattery is like cologne water, to be smelt, not swallowed.

Josh Billings

Life consists not in holding good cards but in playing those you hold well.

Josh Billings

The best time for you to hold your tongue is the time you feel you must say something or bust.

Josh Billings

The best way to convince a fool that he is wrong is to let him have his own way.

Josh Billings

You are one of the forces of nature.

Jules Michelet

I never could be good when I was not happy

Julia Ward Howe

As a rule, men worry more about what they can't see than about what they can.

Julius Caesar

Cowards die many times before their actual deaths.

Julius Caesar

I love the name of honor, more than I fear death.

Julius Caesar

Experience praises the most happy the one who made the most people happy.

Karl Marx

It is even better to act quickly and err than to hesitate until the time of action is past.

Karl Von Clausewitz

The unspoken word never does harm.

Lajos Kossuth

When I let go of what I am, I become what I might be.

Lao Tzu

Violence, even well intentioned, always rebounds upon oneself.

Lao Tzu

To the mind that is still, the whole universe surrenders.

Lao Tzu

To see things in the seed, that is genius.

Lao Tzu

The power of intuitive understanding will protect you from harm until the end of your days.

Lao Tzu

The journey of a thousand miles begins with one step.

Lao Tzu

Respond intelligently even to unintelligent treatment.

Lao Tzu

Mastering others is strength. Mastering yourself is true power.

Lao Tzu

An ant on the move does more than a dozing ox.

Lao Tzu

I am persuaded that every time a man smiles - but much more so when he laughs - it adds something to this fragment of life.

Laurence Sterne

Pain and pleasure, like light and darkness, succeed each other.

Laurence Sterne

Respect for ourselves guides our morals, respect for others guides our manners.

Laurence Sterne

Truth, like gold, is to be obtained not by its growth, but by washing away from it all that is not gold.

Leo Tolstoy

In the name of God, stop a moment, cease your work, look around you.

Leo Tolstoy

The great recipe for success is to work, and always work.

Leon Gambetta

The long term versus the short term argument is one used by losers.

Lord Acton

To be able to look back upon one's past life with satisfaction is to live twice.

Lord Acton

He who believes is strong; he who doubts is weak. Strong convictions precede great actions.

Louisa May Alcott

"Stay" is a charming word in a friend's vocabulary.

Louisa May Alcott

Have regular hours for work and play; make each day both useful and pleasant, and prove that you understand the worth of time by employing it well. Then youth will be delightful, old age will bring few regrets, and life will become a beautiful success.

Louisa May Alcott

You have a good many little gifts and virtues, but there is no need of parading them, for conceit spoils the finest genius. There is not much danger that real talent or goodness will be overlooked long, and the great charm of all power is modesty.

Louisa May Alcott

We all have our own life to pursue, our own kind of dream to be weaving. And we all have the power to make wishes come true, as long as we keep believing.

Louisa May Alcott

A faithful friend is a strong defense; and he that hath found him hath found a treasure.

Louisa May Alcott

Good books, like good friends, are few and chosen; the more select, the more enjoyable.

Louisa May Alcott

Life is my college. May I graduate well, and earn some honors!

Louisa May Alcott

Never use a long word when a short one will do.

Louisa May Alcott

Patience is the art of hoping.

Luc de Clapiers

When a thought is too weak to be expressed simply, it is a proof that it should be rejected.

Luc de Clapiers

Give a man a fish and you feed him for a day; teach a man to fish and you feed him for a lifetime.

Maimonides

Teach thy tongue to say 'I do not know,' and thou shalt progress.

Maimonides

The risk of a wrong decision is preferable to the terror of indecision.

Maimonides

You must accept the truth from whatever source it comes.

Maimonides

Your life is what your thoughts make it.

Marcus Aurelius

You must become an old man in good time if you wish to be an old man long.

Marcus Aurelius

Where a man can live, he can also live well.

Marcus Aurelius

Waste no more time arguing about what a good man should be. Be one.

Marcus Aurelius

Tomorrow is nothing, today is too late; the good lived yesterday.

Marcus Aurelius

Very little is needed to make a happy life; it is all within yourself, in your way of thinking.

Marcus Aurelius

There is nothing happens to any person but what was in his power to go through with.

Marcus Aurelius

The only wealth which you will keep forever is the wealth you have given away.

Marcus Aurelius

The best revenge is to be unlike him who performed the injury.

Marcus Aurelius

That which is not good for the bee-hive cannot be good for the bees.

Marcus Aurelius

Men exist for the sake of one another.

Marcus Aurelius

Look within. Within is the fountain of good, and it will ever bubble up, if thou wilt ever dig.

Marcus Aurelius

Let not your mind run on what you lack as much as on what you have already.

Marcus Aurelius

If it is not right do not do it; if it is not true do not say it.

Marcus Aurelius

Execute every act of thy life as though it were thy last.

Marcus Aurelius

Everything we hear is an opinion, not a fact. Everything we see is a perspective, not the truth.

Marcus Aurelius

 Be content to seem what you really are.

Marcus Aurelius

Anger cannot be dishonest.

Marcus Aurelius

A man's worth is no greater than his ambitions.

Marcus Aurelius

Surely it is much more generous to forgive and remember, than to forgive and forget.

Maria Edgeworth

We are so vain that we even care for the opinion of those we don't care for

Marie von Ebner-Eschenbach

Don't go around saying the world owes you a living. The world owes you nothing. It was here first.

Mark Twain

Age is an issue of mind over matter. If you don't mind, it doesn't matter.

Mark Twain

Kindness is the language which the deaf can hear and the blind can see.

Mark Twain

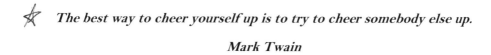 *The best way to cheer yourself up is to try to cheer somebody else up.*

Mark Twain

The greater part of our happiness or misery depends on our dispositions and not our circumstances.

Martha Washington

If we treated everyone we meet with the same affection we bestow upon our favorite cat, they, too, would purr.

Martin Delaney

Even if I knew that tomorrow the world would go to pieces, I would still plant my apple tree.

Martin Luther

Forgiveness is God's command.

Martin Luther

Let the wife make the husband glad to come home, and let him make her sorry to see him leave.

Martin Luther

Peace if possible, truth at all costs.

Martin Luther

Pray, and let God worry.

Martin Luther

You are not only responsible for what you say, but also for what you do not say.

Martin Luther

It is a sign that your reputation is small and sinking if your own tongue must praise you.

Matthew Hale

Pity is treason.

Maximilien Robespierre

All God wants of man is a peaceful heart.

Meister Eckhart

If the only prayer you ever say in your entire life is thank you, it will be enough.

Meister Eckhart

When you are thwarted, it is your own attitude that is out of order.

Meister Eckhart

Friends are the siblings God never gave us.

Mencius

Great is the man who has not lost his childlike heart.

Mencius

Sincerity is the way to heaven.

Mencius

There is no greater delight than to be conscious of sincerity on self-examination.

Mencius

A man who fears suffering is already suffering from what he fears.

Michel de Montaigne

A straight oar looks bent in the water. What matters is not merely that we see things but how we see them.

Michel de Montaigne

Age imprints more wrinkles in the mind than it does on the face.

Michel de Montaigne

Ambition is not a vice of little people.

Michel de Montaigne

He who establishes his argument by noise and command shows that his reason is weak.

Michel de Montaigne

I do myself a greater injury in lying than I do him of whom I tell a lie.

Michel de Montaigne

I study myself more than any other subject. That is my metaphysics, that is my physics.

Michel de Montaigne

Ignorance is the softest pillow on which a man can rest his head.

Michel de Montaigne

It is good to rub and polish our brain against that of others.

Michel de Montaigne

It is not death, it is dying that alarms me.

Michel de Montaigne

Lend yourself to others, but give yourself to yourself.

Michel de Montaigne

Let us not be ashamed to speak what we shame not to think.

Michel de Montaigne

Not being able to govern events, I govern myself.

Michel de Montaigne

Poverty of goods is easily cured; poverty of soul, impossible.

Michel de Montaigne

Stubborn and ardent clinging to one's opinion is the best proof of stupidity.

Michel de Montaigne

The finest souls are those that have the most variety and suppleness.

Michel de Montaigne

The thing I fear most is fear.

Michel de Montaigne

There are some defeats more triumphant than victories.

Michel de Montaigne

In order to attain the impossible, one must attempt the absurd.

Miguel de Cervantes

Never stand begging for that which you have the power to earn.

Miguel de Cervantes

Our greatest foes, and whom we must chiefly combat, are within.

Miguel de Cervantes

Thou hast seen nothing yet.

Miguel de Cervantes

Tis the only comfort of the miserable to have partners in their woes.

Miguel de Cervantes

Truth will rise above falsehood as oil above water.

Miguel de Cervantes

Perceive that which cannot be seen with the eye.

Miyamoto Musashi

Do nothing which is of no use.

Miyamoto Musashi

The analysis of concepts is for the understanding nothing more than what the magnifying glass is for sight.

Moses Mendelssohn

He who fears being conquered is sure of defeat.

Napolean Bonaparte

A picture is worth a thousand words.

Napolean Bonaparte

A true man hates no one.

Napolean Bonaparte

Ability is nothing without opportunity.

Napolean Bonaparte

Death is nothing, but to live defeated and inglorious is to die daily.

Napolean Bonaparte

Glory is fleeting, but obscurity is forever.

Napolean Bonaparte

It requires more courage to suffer than to die.

Napolean Bonaparte

Men take only their needs into consideration - never their abilities.

Napolean Bonaparte

Respect the burden.

Napolean Bonaparte

Riches do not consist in the possession of treasures, but in the use made of them.

Napolean Bonaparte

The best cure for the body is a quiet mind.

Napolean Bonaparte

There is one kind of robber whom the law does not strike at, and who steals what is most precious to men: time.

Napolean Bonaparte

Throw off your worries when you throw off your clothes at night.

Napolean Bonaparte

Get there first with the most.

Nathan Bedford Forrest

Our most intimate friend is not he to whom we show the worst, but the best of our nature.

Nathaniel Hawthorne

Time flies over us, but leaves it shadow behind.

Nathaniel Hawthorne

We must not always talk in the market-place of what happens to us in the forest.

Nathaniel Hawthorne

Just as our eyes need light in order to see, our minds need ideas in order to conceive.

Nicholas Malebranche

Necessity has no law.

Oliver Cromwell

Subtlety may deceive you; integrity never will.

Oliver Cromwell

He who stops being better stops being good.

Oliver Cromwell

The grandest thing has been the lifting up of the gates and the opening of the doors to the women of America, giving liberty to twenty-seven million women, thus opening to them a new and larger life and a higher ideal.

Olympia Brown

The main thing is to make history, not to write it.

Otto von Bismarck

Either I will find a way, or I will make one.

Philip Sidney

Those who give hoping to be rewarded with honor are not giving, they are bargaining.

Philo

The antiquity and general acceptance of an opinion is not assurance of its truth.

Pierre Bayle

The easiest way to be cheated is to believe yourself to be more cunning than others.

Pierre Charron

I am more exempt and more distant than any man in the world.

Pierre de Fermat

Hardly any human being is capable of pursuing two professions or two arts rightly

Plato

We are twice armed if we fight with faith.

Plato

The beginning is the most important part of the work.

Plato

A good decision is based on knowledge and not on numbers.

Plato

All the gold which is under or upon the earth is not enough to give in exchange for virtue.

Plato

Any man may easily do harm, but not every man can do good to another.

Plato

 Be kind, for everyone you meet is fighting a hard battle.

Plato

Better a little which is well done, than a great deal imperfectly.

Plato

Death is not the worst that can happen to men.

Plato

For a man to conquer himself is the first and noblest of all victories.

Plato

Good actions give strength to ourselves and inspire good actions in others.

Plato

I shall assume that your silence gives consent.

Plato

It is right to give every man his due.

Plato

Justice means minding one's own business and not meddling with other men's concerns.

Plato

Knowledge becomes evil if the aim be not virtuous.

Plato

Knowledge is true opinion.

Plato

Let parents bequeath to their children not riches, but the spirit of reverence.

Plato

 Life must be lived as play.

Plato

No law or ordinance is mightier than understanding.

Plato

Nothing in the affairs of men is worthy of great anxiety.

Plato

There is no harm in repeating a good thing.

Plato

A few vices are sufficient to darken many virtues.

Plutarch

He is not wise to me who is wise in words only, but he who is wise in deeds.

Pope Gregory I

There are two sides to every question.

Protagoras

Man is the measure of all things, of things that are that they are, and of things that are not that they are not.

Protagoras

The important thing is not what they think of me, but what I think of them.

Queen Victoria

Whilst we deliberate how to begin a thing, it grows too late to begin it.

Quintilian

While we are examining into everything we sometimes find truth where we least expected it.

Quintilian

We excuse our sloth under the pretext of difficulty.

Quintilian

Those who wish to appear wise among fools, among the wise seem foolish.

Quintilian

A true friend is somebody who can make us do what we can.

Ralph Waldo Emerson

Don't be too timid and squeamish about your actions. All life is an experiment.

Ralph Waldo Emerson

Enthusiasm is the mother of effort, and without it nothing great was ever achieved.

Ralph Waldo Emerson

For every minute you remain angry, you give up sixty seconds of peace of mind.

Ralph Waldo Emerson

Fear defeats more people than any other one thing in the world.

Ralph Waldo Emerson

The only way to have a friend is to be one.

Ralph Waldo Emerson

Write it on your heart that every day is the best day in the year.

Ralph Waldo Emerson

A man is usually more careful of his money than he is of his principles.

Ralph Waldo Emerson

If you want to go east, don't go west.

Ramakrishna

Each man must grant himself the emotions that he needs and the morality that suits him.

Remy de Gourmont

A minute's success pays the failure of years.

Robert Browning

Good, to forgive; best to forget.

Robert Browning

Do your duty in all things. You cannot do more, you should never wish to do less.

Robert E. Lee

Never do a wrong thing to make a friend or to keep one.

Robert E. Lee

Anger is a wind which blows out the lamp of the mind.

Robert Ingersoll

Few rich men own their own property. The property owns them.

Robert Ingersoll

Hope is the only bee that makes honey without flowers.

Robert Ingersoll

I am the inferior of any man whose rights I trample under foot.

Robert Ingersoll

I would rather live and love where death is king than have eternal life where love is not.

Robert Ingersoll

If I owe Smith ten dollars and God forgives me, that doesn't pay Smith.

Robert Ingersoll

Kindness is the sunshine in which virtue grows.

Robert Ingersoll

More people are flattered into virtue than bullied out of vice.

Robert Smith Surtee

A book is the only immortality.

Rufus Choate

Conscience is the authentic voice of God to you.

Rutherford B. Hayes

Do not let your bachelor ways crystallize so that you can't soften them when you come to have a wife and a family of your own.

Rutherford B. Hayes

When in Rome, live as the Romans do; when elsewhere, live as they live elsewhere.

Saint Ambrose

This is the very perfection of a man, to find out his own imperfections.

Saint Augustine

Hear the other side.

Saint Augustine

Teach us to give and not to count the cost.

Saint Ignatius

The scars of others should teach us caution.

Saint Jerome

The friendship that can cease has never been real.

Saint Jerome

Never look a gift horse in the mouth.

Saint Jerome

Keep doing some kind of work, that the devil may always find you employed.

Saint Jerome

Pain is never permanent.

Saint Teresa of Avila

Be gentle to all and stern with yourself.

Saint Teresa of Avila

A good man would prefer to be defeated than to defeat injustice by evil means.

Sallust

All who consult on doubtful matters, should be void of hatred, friendship, anger, and pity.

Sallust

Do as much as possible, and talk of yourself as little as possible

Sallust

Think like a man of action, and act like a man of thought.

Sallust

It is much easier to find fault with others, than to be faultless ourselves.

Samuel Richardson

It may be very generous in one person to offer what it would be ungenerous in another to accept.

Samuel Richardson

Nothing dries sooner than tears.

Samuel Richardson

The companion of an evening, and the companion for life, require very different qualifications.

Samuel Richardson

Those we dislike can do nothing to please us.

Samuel Richardson

Grace tried is better than grace, and more than grace; it is glory in its infancy.

Samuel Rutherford

I am convinced that life is 10% what happens to me and 96% how I react to it.

Scipio Africanus

Wisdom begins in wonder.

Socrates

The unexamined life is not worth living.

Socrates

The greatest way to live with honor in this world is to be what we pretend to be.

Socrates

It is not living that matters, but living rightly.

Socrates

Beware the barrenness of a busy life.

Socrates

It is the mind that makes the body.

Sojourner Truth

Truth is powerful and it prevails.

Sojourner Truth

Face the facts of being what you are, for that is what changes what you are.

Soren Kierkegaard

Life can only be understood backwards; but it must be lived forwards.

Soren Kierkegaard

Once you label me you negate me.

Soren Kierkegaard

Our life always expresses the result of our dominant thoughts.

Soren Kierkegaard

To dare is to lose one's footing momentarily. Not to dare is to lose oneself.

Soren Kierkegaard

Trouble is the common denominator of living. It is the great equalizer.

Soren Kierkegaard

Man's heart away from nature becomes hard.

Standing Bear

Those who have happy homes seldom turn out badly.

Stonewall Jackson

The general who wins the battle makes many calculations in his temple before the battle is fought. The general who loses makes but few calculations beforehand.

Sun Tzu

Opportunities multiply as they are seized.

Sun Tzu

You have to believe in yourself.

Sun Tzu

Can you imagine what I would do if I could do all I can?

Sun Tzu

The older I get, the greater power I seem to have to help the world; I am like a snowball - the further I am rolled the more I gain.

Susan B. Anthony

Things forbidden have a secret charm.

Tacitus

Live your life that the fear of death can never enter your heart.

Tecumseh

Show respect to all people, but grovel to none.

Tecumseh

The books that help you the most are those which make you think the most.

Theodore Parker

Remorse is the pain of sin.

Theodore Parker

Outward judgment often fails, inward judgment never.

Theodore Parker

Never violate the sacredness of your individual self-respect.

Theodore Parker

Let others laugh when you sacrifice desire to duty, if they will. You have time and eternity to rejoice in.

Theodore Parker

I am a part of everything that I have read.

Theodore Roosevelt

If you could kick the person in the pants responsible for most of your trouble, you wouldn't sit for a month.

Theodore Roosevelt

The most important single ingredient in the formula of success is knowing how to get along with people.

Theodore Roosevelt

Far and away the best prize that life has to offer is the chance to work hard at work worth doing.

Theodore Roosevelt

I keep my good health by having a very bad temper, kept under good control.

Theodore Roosevelt

Great thoughts speak only to the thoughtful mind, but great actions speak to all mankind.

Theodore Roosevelt

In life as in a football game, the principle to follow is: Hit the line hard.

Theodore Roosevelt

Time is the most valuable thing a man can spend.

Theophrastus

The man of petty ambition if invited to dinner will be eager to be set next his host.

Theophrastus

The things that we love tell us what we are.

Thomas Aquinas

A man lives by believing something: not by debating and arguing about many things.

Thomas Carlyle

A strong mind always hopes, and has always cause to hope.

Thomas Carlyle

Be not a slave of words.

Thomas Carlyle

Conviction is worthless unless it is converted into conduct.

Thomas Carlyle

Do the duty which lies nearest to you, the second duty will then become clearer.

Thomas Carlyle

I do not believe in the collective wisdom of individual ignorance.

Thomas Carlyle

I've got a great ambition to die of exhaustion rather than boredom.

Thomas Carlyle

If what you have done is unjust, you have not succeeded.

Thomas Carlyle

Make yourself an honest man, and then you may be sure there is one less rascal in the world. No amount of ability is of the slightest avail without honor.

Thomas Carlyle

No pressure, no diamonds.

Thomas Carlyle

Nothing builds self-esteem and self-confidence like accomplishment.

Thomas Carlyle

Nothing is more terrible than activity without insight.

Thomas Carlyle

One must verify or expel his doubts, and convert them into the certainty of Yes or NO.

Thomas Carlyle

Our main business is not to see what lies dimly at a distance,but to do what lies clearly at hand.

Thomas Carlyle

Silence is more eloquent than words.

Thomas Carlyle

The first duty of man is to conquer fear; he must get rid of it, he cannot act till then.

Thomas Carlyle

The greatest of all faults, I should say, is to be conscious of none.

Thomas Carlyle

There are good and bad times, but our mood changes more often than our fortune.

Thomas Carlyle

Work alone is noble.

Thomas Carlyle

Charity begins at home, but should not end there.

Thomas Fuller

Two things a man should never be angry at: what he can help, and what he cannot help.

Thomas Fuller

One may miss the mark by aiming too high as too low.

Thomas Fuller

Be a friend to thyself, and others will be so too.

Thomas Fuller

Better be alone than in bad company.

Thomas Fuller

Bad excuses are worse than none

Thomas Fuller

No man's error becomes his own Law; nor obliges him to persist in it.

Thomas Hobbes

Those who have happy homes seldom turn out badly.

Thomas J. Jackson

Those who have happy homes seldom turn out badly.

Thomas Jefferson

A coward is much more exposed to quarrels than a man of spirit.

Thomas Jefferson

An injured friend is the bitterest of foes.

Thomas Jefferson

Honesty is the first chapter in the book of wisdom.

Thomas Jefferson

Only aim to do your duty, and mankind will give you credit where you fail.

Thomas Jefferson

The glow of one warm thought is to me worth more than money.

Thomas Jefferson

When angry count to ten before you speak. If very angry, count to one hundred

Thomas Jefferson

Ignorance is bold and knowledge reserved.

Thucydides

We secure our friends not by accepting favors but by doing them.

Thucydides

What we gave, we have; What we spent, we had; What we left, we lost.

Tyron Edwards

To rule one's anger is well; to prevent it is better.

Tyron Edwards

Right actions in the future are the best apologies for bad actions in the past.

Tyron Edwards

People never improve unless they look to some standard or example higher or better than themselves.

Tyron Edwards

He that never changes his opinion never corrects mistakes and will never be wiser on the morrow than he is today.

Tyron Edwards

Between two evils, choose neither; between two goods, choose both.

Tyron Edwards

Ignorance is the primary source of all misery and vice.

Victor Cousin

You may not realize it when it happens, but a kick in the teeth may be the best thing in the world for you.

Walt Disney

Laughter is America's most important export.

Walt Disney

The way to get started is to quit talking and begin doing.

Walt Disney

A man should never neglect his family for business.

Walt Disney

When you're curious, you find lots of interesting things to do.

Walt Disney

If you can dream it, you can do it.

Walt Disney

It's kind of fun to do the impossible.

Walt Disney

Get a good idea and stay with it. Do it, and work at it until it's done right.

Walt Disney

Do what you do so well that they will want to see it again and bring their friends

Walt Disney

For success, attitude is equally as important as ability.

Walter Scott

O, what a tangled web we weave when first we practise to deceive!

Walter Scott

Of all vices, drinking is the most incompatible with greatness.

Walter Scott

We build statues out of snow, and weep to see them melt.

Walter Scott

Age is a matter of feeling, not of years.

Washington Irving

One of the greatest and simplest tools for learning more and growing is doing more.

Washington Irving

 A tart temper never mellows with age, and a sharp tongue is the only edged tool that grows keener with constant use.

Washington Irving

The best education in the world is that got by struggling to get a living.

Wendell Phillips

Better a bad excuse, than none at all.

William Camden

The early bird catches the worm.

William Camden

You never know what you can do till you try.

William Cobbett

Tact is one of the first mental virtues, the absence of it is fatal to the best talent.

William Gilmore Simms

The dread of criticism is the death of genius.

William Gilmore Simms

The only true source of politeness is consideration.

William Gilmore Simms

Men are apt to mistake the strength of their feeling for the strength of their argument. The heated mind resents the chill touch and relentless scrutiny of logic.

William Gladstone

Selfishness is the greatest curse of the human race.

William Gladstone

The disease of an evil conscience is beyond the practice of all the physicians of all the countries in the world.

William Gladstone

You cannot fight against the future. Time is on our side.

William Gladstone

I am naturally taciturn, and became a silent and attentive listener.

William Hamilton Maxwell

A chain is no stronger than its weakest link, and life is after all a chain.

William James

A man has as many social selves as there are individuals who recognize him.

William James

Act as if what you do makes a difference. It does.

William James

Action may not bring happiness but there is no happiness without action.

William James

Begin to be now what you will be hereafter.

William James

Everybody should do at least two things each day that he hates to do, just for practice.

William James

If you want a quality, act as if you already had it.

William James

In business for yourself, not by yourself.

William James

In the dim background of mind we know what we ought to be doing but somehow we cannot start.

William James

Most people never run far enough on their first wind to find out they've got a second.

William James

Nothing is so fatiguing as the eternal hanging on of an uncompleted task.

William James

The best argument I know for an immortal life is the existence of a man who deserves one.

William James

The great use of life is to spend it for something that will outlast it.

William James

The greatest weapon against stress is our ability to choose one thought over another.

William James

To change ones life: Start immediately. Do it flamboyantly.

William James

We don't laugh because we're happy - we're happy because we laugh.

William James

When you have to make a choice and don't make it, that is in itself a choice.

William James

Take care of the pence, for the pounds will take care of themselves.

William Lowndes

A good laugh is sunshine in the house.

William Makepeace Thackeray

Bravery never goes out of fashion.

William Makepeace Thackeray

Good humor is one of the best articles of dress one can wear in society.

William Makepeace Thackeray

I would rather make my name than inherit it.

William Makepeace Thackeray

It is best to love wisely, no doubt; but to love foolishly is better than not to be able to love at all.

William Makepeace Thackeray

There are many sham diamonds in this life which pass for real, and vice versa.

William Makepeace Thackeray

In the time of darkest defeat, victory may be nearest.

William McKinley

That's all a man can hope for during his lifetime - to set an example - and when he is dead, to be an inspiration for history.

William McKinley

It is vain to do with more what can be done with fewer.

William of Ockham

Avoid popularity; it has many snares, and no real benefit.

William Penn

Humility and knowledge in poor clothes excel pride and ignorance in costly attire.

William Penn

The jealous are troublesome to others, but a torment to themselves.

William Penn

A thousand acres that can feed a thousand souls is better than ten thousand acres of no more effect.

William Petty

Confidence is a plant of slow growth in an aged heart.

William Pitt

We are what we repeatedly do. Excellence, then, is not an act, it is a habit.

William Prescott

Whatever you have, spend less.

William Samuel Johnson

To keep your secret is wisdom; to expect others to keep it is folly.

William Samuel Johnson

How poor are they who have not patience! What wound did ever heal but by degrees.

William Shakespeare

Ill deeds are doubled with an evil word.

William Shakespeare

Strong reasons make strong actions.

William Shakespeare

It is not enough to help the feeble up, but to support him after.

William Shakespeare

No legacy is so rich as honesty.

William Shakespeare

Love all, trust a few, do wrong to none.

William Shakespeare

Courage - a perfect sensibility of the measure of danger, and a mental willingness to endure it.

William Tecumseh Sherman

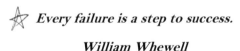 *Every failure is a step to success.*

William Whewell

I have often repented speaking, but never of holding my tongue.

Xenocrates

Fast is fine, but accuracy is everything.

Xenophon

Those whose character is mean and vicious will rouse others to animosity against them.

Xun Zi

The person attempting to travel two roads at once will get nowhere.

Xun Zi

Pride and excess bring disaster for man.

Xun Zi

I once tried thinking for an entire day, but I found it less valuable than one moment of study.

Xun Zi

I have always done my duty. I am ready to die. My only regret is for the friends I leave behind me.

Zachary Taylor

Made in the USA
Lexington, KY
07 December 2010